‘I Reme
Was .

Ron Brown

THE STORY OF HAYLING ISLAND

Down Memory Lane

Down Memory Lane I linger long,
Till evening shadows fall,
To dream of golden days bygone,
And radiant hours recall.

Sponsored by
Millers of Hayling

MILESTONE PUBLICATIONS

Phototypesetting by Inforum Ltd, Portsmouth
Printed in Great Britain by Conifer Press, Fareham, Hampshire

Published by Milestone Publications,
62 Murray Road, Horndean, Hants PO8 9JL

First impression 1983
Reprinted 1984, 1985

British Library Cataloguing in Publication Data

Brown, Ron, *1932–*
"I remember when it was just fields": the story of Hayling Island. — 2nd ed. — (Down memory lane; 3)
1. Hayling Island (England) — Social life and customs
I. Title II. Series
942.2′795 DA670.H3

ISBN 0-903852-17-9

Sponsored by Millers of Hayling Island

"I REMEMBER WHEN IT WAS JUST FIELDS".
The Story of Hayling Island

At the turn of this century Hayling Island was a very different place to what it is today. It was well-endowed with small farms providing milk, vegetables, flour and other necessities for the Islanders. There must be many senior residents who really can say "I remember when it was just fields".

Although this book about Hayling is primarily concerned with life and events within living memory, it is useful to have a brief history of the Island to understand its progress over the years. There is little evidence of early Britons living on the Island. They preferred to make their settlements near freshwater streams surrounded by the good pasture land for cattle that river valleys afforded. Locally the Meon Valley and Itchen Valley were inhabited by early tribes, due to the presence of fresh water. Before the Romans invaded Britain, the Britons were making good progress with pottery, weaving and dying, mining and metal work. They had a coinage system and had even built chariots.

The Romans first invaded Britain in 54 B.C., landing in Dover and heading for London. It was not until 43 A.D. that they completed the task of conquering Britain completely. Over the years many examples of Roman occupation of Hayling have been unearthed, and a large earthen fortress at Tourner Bury has been attributed to them, although another opinion is that the works were pre-Roman, and similar to those described by Caesar as the "oppida" of the Britons, serving as tribal places for refuge and defence.

In the early 1800s pottery of Roman origin was found in the Towncil Field, in the northern part of the Island, the name Towncil being a corruption of town council. During the last century the finding of coins was quite a regular occurrence in this area and so were the sounds of farmers cursing, for their ploughs were always hitting buried walls and hidden stones. This rubble was unearthed and used to mend the roads in days gone by.

Then in 1897 an enthusiastic archaeologist named Dr. Talfourd Ely became interested in the Towncil site. After obtaining the permission and backing of the field's owner, William Carpenter Turner, the doctor began digging in earnest. The historical treasures that his spade uncovered over the following eight years or so would suggest that the Romans held Hayling in very high esteem, for along with the discovery of pottery, mosaics, charcoal urns and nails, Ely found the foundations of domestic buildings and a basilica some 130 feet long, complete with drains and an extensive system of chambers and corridors of some size. Amongst the varied array of coins, keys, knives and bangles unearthed, one exciting find was a bronze and blue enamel brooch. Animal remains were quite common, the tusks of wild boar in particular. By 1905, Dr. Talfourd Ely was well into his 60s. The amount of spadework required for this arduous task was proving too much for him so he retired. He had certainly earned a rest after his invaluable efforts.

There is not much evidence that either the Saxons or the Danes troubled with Hayling when they invaded Britain. It is known that they came to Bosham, and possibly they explored the Island's sheltered creeks and extensive woodland. In 1920 a stone club was found in the Eastoke area during a fierce gale in which a sand dune was shifted by the wind, thus uncovering the weapon for the first time in hundreds of years. The wooden shaft of the club was in a very good state of preservation and the stone portion typical of the type used by Saxon soldiers.

One of the earliest references to Hayling occurred in 1045 when the manor was presented to the monks of Winchester by Queen Emma. She had been a beautiful princess, marrying King

A pleasant rural scene of yesteryear in Manor Road

Ethelred the Unready in 1002, then following his death in 1016, she married King Canute. She had the distinction of being the wife of two Kings, and the mother of two Kings. Unfortunately she was rather harshly treated by one of the latter, King Edward the Confessor. He thought that she had hindered his accession to the throne, so he trumped up a murder charge against her. The story goes that Emma demanded a public trial, and elected to take part in an "ordeal by fire" in order to prove her innocence. She strolled across nine red-hot ploughshares placed in Winchester Cathedral, and despite the fact that she put her full weight on them, she completed the course without batting an eyelid! Her dastardly son Edward was immediately prompted into prostrating himself at his mother's feet and begging for forgiveness. It was following this miraculous act that the Queen bestowed nine manors on the Winchester monks, one of them being the manor of Hayling, also known as Haylynge, Heilinciga or Halinger during that period. Despite the toughness of her feet, Queen Emma only survived seven years after her ordeal by fire, dying in 1052.

The Norman Conquest altered Hayling's history considerably, after William had defeated Harold with his "arrow in the sky" battle tactics projecting arrows almost vertically upwards so that the missiles fell down on the heads of the British warriors. William presented Hayling to the Abbey of Jumieges in France, along with many other rich lands. The gift of Hayling caused trouble between Winchester and Jumieges and the matter was decided to some extent by another monarch, Henry I, who favoured Jumieges and helped them to procure a renewal of their original grant.

In the following years Henry II also looked kindly upon the Jumieges monks, granting them free warren in Hayling as Henry I had done before him. He also allowed them to carry all things from the province of the church freely to all the ports of England and Normandy, so it would seem that the Hayling monks carried on a lucrative export business. Although the Abbot and monks of Jumieges were allowed to exercise almost dictatorial powers on the Island, it must be said that under their guidance the people of Hayling spent a considerable period in peace and tranquility, whilst much of the country was riven with strife.

Henry V was carrying out a policy of taking over any priories that enjoyed foreign backing and in 1414 he granted Hayling to his new foundation, the Carthusian Priory of Sheen in Surrey. It remained peaceful until Henry VIII came to power and dissolved all monasteries following a disagreement with the Pope regarding the sanctity of the marriage vow. Sheen Priory surrendered in 1539 and in 1541 Henry part-exchanged the Hayling Manor and the site of Hayling Priory with Holy Trinity College of Arundel in exchange for the Manor of Bury in Sussex. A few years later the college was granted to Henry Fitzalan, Earl of Arundel, whose only son died without an heir, with the result that the Manor of Hayling was bequeathed to one of Henry Fitzalan's sons-in-law, John Lord Lumley. During the reign of Queen Elizabeth I, the then Earl of Arundel purchased the Hayling lands from Lord Lumley, and from that date they remained under the control of the successive Dukes of Norfolk until 1825.

Padwick The Powerful.

The year 1825 proved to be one of the most significant in the history of the Island, for it heralded the arrival of William Padwick who on 24 February purchased the manor, rectory, and estates from Bernard Edward, Duke of Norfolk, the acquisition being obtained through an Act of Parliament. Described in the *Victoria County History* as a distinguished lawyer, Padwick had dreams of developing Hayling into a coastal resort that would rival Brighton, and only two years prior to his 1825 take-over he had helped to form a company to promote the building of a bridge to link the Island with Langston in the Parish of Havant. The Duke of Norfolk and Sir George Staunton of Leigh Park joined Padwick as the three principal shareholders in the company, but although the Duke officially opened the bridge, by that time he had lost interest in the future of Hayling, hence the change of power in 1825.

Assuming his role as Lord of the Manor, William Padwick certainly lived up to the title, and things could never be described as dull while he was around, for in the following thirty years or so he kept the courtrooms busy by bringing several suits against his tenants in connection with liberties of the Manor. Although he ruled with a rod of iron, and generally emerged victor in his long-running battles with the Island's residents, he came unstuck in 1846 when he commenced legal proceedings against the burgesses of Portsmouth. This concerned a piece of land known as "Howard's Furlong" in the Parish of Portsea, in the neighbourhood of the canal, an area covered in houses. William claimed that the land was part of his manor, and had no fewer than 600 separate acts of ejectment issued in order to recover it. The good folk of Portsea were extremely worried, and feared that they would lose all they had in the world, namely their humble abodes. However, at a High Court hearing in Exeter, Justice Coleridge ruled against Padwick. Not one to take defeat lightly, William appealed to the House of Lords, but this also went against him.

The Lord of the Manor must have a Manor House, hence the resplendent building that dominated the centre of the Island. Built in the Georgian style, it was erected in 1777 for Edward Duke of Norfolk, and within its noble structure it boasted a Court Room where manor business was conducted. The Manor House stood on the site of the former Grange, an ancient building that served as the residence of the Steward who looked after the agricultural requirements of the local monks, the grounds were surrounded by a moat. The dovecotes that are associated with the Manor House were of a much earlier origin, reputed to be some of the oldest structures of their kind to be erected in this country. Hundreds of doves provided eggs and roasting poultry. The famous Manor Barn, also very old, was a most curious building indeed, built with wood obtained from a German boat that was wrecked on the Hayling shores many centuries ago. The story goes that the cargo of oak timbers was en-route from the Elbe to France, intended for a monastry to be erected there.

William Padwick died in 1861, leaving three daughters and one son, and as so very often occurs following the death of a person of property, family differences arose. Eventually the greater part of the manor was disenfranchised, with the estate passing into the hands of Mr. Osmond Barnard in 1870, then taken over by Mr. J.C. Park in 1871, and subsequently taken on by his son Mr. C.J. Park in 1887. Although Hayling Manor was the largest and thus featured more prominently in historical works, there were two other ancient manors in the form of Havant Manor in the north of the Island, and the Manor of Northstoke, Eastoke and Westhay, which was divided into the north and south parishes. During the last century Sir Frederick Fitzwygram of Leigh Park was one of the much respected Lords of Havant Manor. Northstoke, Eastoke and Westhay Manor, passed from the Earls of Sussex into families with names such as Latelais, Peckham, Peckham-Williams, Penfold, Hollest, and eventually to Thomas Harris of Donnington in 1845. Harris sold it to Mr. Lynch White of Streatham in 1870, who in turn sold the estate in building plots in 1890, the largest of which was purchased by Mr. Frank Pearce. Pearce was a most colourful character indeed, he was the proprietor of the People's Palace music hall in Portsmouth's Lake Road, which later became the

The library, which used to stand in front of Norfolk Crescent

St. Peter's Church, Northney

St. Mary's Church, South Hayling

The Salterns, Mengham Rythe

The Old Bathing House, Beachlands

well-loved Palladium picture house. Frank Pearce commands several paragraphs in another book in the "Down Memory Lane" series, the best-selling *Cinemas of Portsmouth*.

Praising the Lord in Hayling

In most written works and guide-books about one specific town or place, it will be noted that places of worship appear to dominate most of the history, but Hayling is an exception. In fact some guides covering Hampshire only mention the churches at North Hayling and at South Hayling.

Very few books on old Hampshire mention Hayling's first church, and this is quite understandable, for very little is known about it. Even the exact location of the old church is in doubt, opinions vary considerably. The most logical place to site a church that would serve an island would be in the centre, but Trigg's Guide of 1892 theorises that it was situated in the beach area at the south of the Island. The particular area in mind was the Church Rocks, and although the Old Church is reputed to have been overwhelmed and swept away by storms in 1321, this location was the cause of many stories over the years, with tales about the sound of ghostly bells ringing from the depths of the sea. However, wherever the church was situated, it is thought to have been erected in the 1040–50 period.

Around 1826, an ancient font was found in a well in the South Parish, and was thought to be a relic of the first church. Thankfully, it was preserved and resited in South Hayling Church, St. Mary's, referred to as South Hayling Church and dedicated to Our Lady. It is a fine building in the Early English mode, consisting of nave and chancel with a central tower and an oak-shingled spire.

Church roofs are generally a touchy subject with worshippers, for there always seems to be a never ending appeal for funds to repair them. The roof area of St. Mary's provides a daunting prospect for renovation, for it comprises a goodly number of tiles, but in 1933 good sense prevailed when Stares Farm was being demolished to make way for new development. The tiles were found to be in such good condition that they were utilized for the repair of St. Mary's roof. The church is entered through a fine 15th Century porch, but to enter the church grounds one must pass through a charming lychgate, which was erected as a memorial to the First World War dead. It is interesting to note that stocks were once sited adjacent to this gate.

Dominating the churchyard of St. Mary's stands the magnificent yew tree, a sample of nature's work that Islanders have always taken great pride in. Indeed in 1929 they created quite an uproar because the Hayling Yew was not mentioned in the county list of yews, yet with a girth of 33 feet, against Corhampton with 22 feet, Bedhampton with 20 feet, and Warblington with 26 feet, it was by far the largest. Colonel Sandeman took a keen interest in the tree, at his own expense he had it attended by experts from Kew Gardens, and had it railed for protection.

When one surveys the peace and tranquility of the churchyard, it is not surprising to learn that many folk who may have moved away from the area express a wish to be buried there. One such person was Canon James Bell, who was Vicar of Hayling from 1881 to 1889, and although he moved on to higher things and became a Canon at Norwich Cathedral, he never forgot the kindness of the Hayling people and his happy times on the Island. He was granted his wish to be buried at St. Mary's when he died in 1934 at the age of 78. I am sure one of Canon Bell's fondest memories must have been of the fine choir at the church, and in particular the voice of William King. William sang until his death at the age of 87 in 1933, and was in fact a chorister at St. Mary's for over 70 years. His longevity could no doubt be attributed to his life in the open air as a gardener at Richmond House for over forty years.

One gentleman of the cloth whom I am sure will still be remembered by many older readers was the Rev. C. Clarke, who served at the church in the early part of this century. Apart from his many good works, one of the highlights of Hayling's social calendar was the splendid New Year's dinner that he and his good lady wife provided each year for the widows of the Island which generally included a decorated tree, presents for everyone, and a jolly good sing-song!

The second notable church is St. Peter's in North Hayling, which was established in the middle of the 12th Century and is possibly some fifty years or so older than South Hayling Church. Referred to as the Chapel of St. Peter at Northwood in Hayling, this church is chiefly in the Early English style, consisting of a nave, chancel, and north transept with a timber belfry above the eastern bay of the nave.

Observed from the exterior, it has the appearance of everything we might expect from a church sited in a pleasant rural village such as North Hayling. Indeed, both the church and its surroundings appear to have remained untouched by the ravages of modern living. However, a couple of hundred years ago, the village of North Hayling was almost entirely destroyed by a dreadful fire which occurred in the 1750s. Aided by a strong wind, the fire reduced village dwellings to ashes within a few hours, the only blessing was that the beloved St. Peter's emerged unscathed. Apart from the spire, the chief features of the exterior of the church are the huge buttresses supporting the east end. Whilst the churchyard has a number of 18th Century tombstones that are worthy of note the reader is referred to White's Directory of 1859 which tells of parish life in the 1840's and 50's.

It is natural that folk in the northern part of the Island should want to be buried at St. Peter's, and not in the parish of South Hayling. This caused quite a stir in the 1920s when a widow from the north objected to her husband being buried in the south, the reason for this being that at that particular time there was no room in the graveyard of North Hayling Church. In 1934 a burial took place at North Hayling that could only be described as unique, it concerned a tramp who was given a funeral worthy of a king! Jimmy Usher was a gentleman of the road who was well liked by the villagers of North Hayling, especially by the children, and it was through this association that Jimmy earnt the title of "The Children's Friend". Not having any relatives, when he died he would have had a pauper's burial, but the whole village made a collection, including many pennies from his young admirers, and he was provided with a marvellous "send-off".

Many years before a road bridge existed to connect Hayling with the mainland, those inhabitants who favoured the Independent form of worship had to walk to Havant in order to pray at the old chapel in The Pallant. This they did by using the Wade Way or the Northern Ferry. They suffered this for a number of years, then in 1811 a move was made to allow the Congregationalists to worship on home ground, and services were held for the first time in a kitchen at Mr. Catterel's farmhouse at Stoke. Gradually, there was enough interest and support to consider the erection of a permanent chapel, and a small plot of land at the corner of Hollow Lane and Elm Grove was obtained. Building began almost immediately, with women and children scouting the beach for suitable materials, the walls being built from rocks, sand and gravel from the shore. Originally it was a low one-roomed structure, but in the following years it was extended considerably. It would be true to say that the new congregational church was not exactly welcomed by members of the other religions on Hayling, and at times the doors of the chapel had to be protected by sheets of iron against bombardment by bricks and other missiles, but the followers of

Monlas Place, North Hayling, 1904

Manor House, c. 1905

The Pound, St. Mary's Road, South Hayling

The Crescent

Beachlands, early 30s

the Church would not be moved and eventually their faith prevailed. In the following pages I shall mention again Mr. W.T. Stead, the famous journalist who was an ardent Congregationalist and worshipped regularly at the Hayling Chapel. Although there cannot be many residents left who can remember Stead, I am sure that there are many who will remember those wonderful temperance rallies of the pre-war years, in which hundreds of children assembled at the Congregational Hall for that annual highlight in the Island's calendar known as the "Little White Ribboners Rally".

Are there any residents who can recall that June day in 1925 when the famous "Woodbine Willie" came to Hayling? His real name was the Rev. Studdert Kennedy, and he was Chaplain to the King. He certainly drew them to the Hayling Kinema, for hundreds turned up to hear him preach. The Church of St. Patrick was erected in 1926 for those of the Roman Catholic faith on the Island, and around that period the Plymouth Brethren also flourished in their own hall.

Earning a Crust

It cannot be said that Hayling has attracted the attention of large industrial undertakings to any great degree, and of course the limited access to this bell-shaped island has not helped. Not wishing to experience the delights of huge juggernauts rumbling through their narrow lanes, it is understandable that the Island's residents have remained content to observe industrial estates mushroom in neighbouring Havant, Fareham and Portsmouth. However, in bygone years Hayling Island was noted for a number of small industries in which its inhabitants could earn a crust or two.

Until the latter half of the last century the making of salt featured prominently in Hayling's export trade, in fact it was famous for its superiority in the foreign markets. The extensive salt works on the Island were mentioned in the Domesday Survey, and it is probable that the product was manufactured here long before the Norman Conquest. Clarke's 1836 Guidebook to Hayling devotes considerable space to the salt industry, and it is interesting to recall the method of manufacture.

The making of salt depended a good deal on the weather, the best time being in the four months of summer. Firstly, the salt seawater was let into brine-pans, which were square shallow places formed in a field adjoining the sea. In fine weather the salt water became brine in approximately seven days, it was then pumped into reservoirs or pits, each holding enough to make some 25 tons of salt. The pumping operation was achieved by a wind-pump fitted with sails. The brine was then transferred as required into pans that were heated in a boiler house, the boiling operation lasting for twelve hours, during which it was skimmed twice. When the salt was formed it was shovelled out hot and wet into wooden troughs that had holes in the bottom, through these ran a dross that was referred to as "bitters". The crystalization of Epsom Salts was formed from these "bitters". After the salt had drained in the troughs for about ten hours it was removed to a storehouse to be made ready for distribution. It was estimated that around 150 tons of salt were produced during the season at Hayling, selling for sixty shillings a ton.

Clarke's guide treated the making of salt on the Island as a tourist attraction, advising visitors that the best time to inspect the boiling-house was at one o'clock in the afternoon, this being the time when the boiling process was nearly completed. I would not have thought that the presence of visitors would be particularly welcomed by the salt workers, for it was jolly hard work with long hours, even if the main season did only take place for four months of the year. It could be said that the Cole family were the "salt of the earth", for this is the name that was linked synonymously with the manufacture of salt in Hayling. Ebenezar Cole was one of the last, if not the last, salt-maker on the Island, beginning as a mere lad by working for his father, George Cole, for the princely sum of two shillings a week. The salt works covered some ten acres, so Ebenezar was kept busy, not only with his involvement in production, as he was also called upon to deliver bags of salt to customers. This he did by horse and cart, travelling to Portsmouth and various other parts of the region. Hayling folk soon caught on to the fact that once Ebenezar had delivered his load, the cart returned to the Island empty, so they asked him to bring things back for them from the outside world. Ebenezar did this quite willingly, for a small fee of course, and the service developed into a flourishing carrying business. Sometimes he would have to swop his faithful old horse for a boat, this was when he was called upon to transport salt to Bosham. The hard working life could not have done Ebenezar Cole much harm, for he passed away at the ripe old age of 90 in 1934. Sadly, Hayling's salt industry had died long before this.

William Derben passed away a year before Ebenezar Cole, he was 82, and his death severed a link with another one of Hayling's old industries, that of brickmaking. The bricks were produced on a site near Tournerbury established about 1840, utilising the excellent brick earth found there. The industry used about fourteen acres of ground and this land was let to John Derben. The bricks produced here were of a very high standard and millions of them were sent to the Isle of Wight and West Worthing. They generally enjoyed a good deal of popularity on the South Coast, for as well as being used for the construction of domestic dwellings, they were also used in Portsmouth Dockyard during the last century in particular for the building of the vast basins there.

From Hayling bricks we move to Hayling oysters, for the local beds were acclaimed in the last century as being the largest and best constructed in England, with huge quantities being sent all over the country from Hayling. It would appear that the oyster merchants did well, for the White's Directory of 1859 lists three of this select band, William Crouch of Sinar, John Gamble of Milton and David Russell of Farlington. The Directory of 1878 only lists one, this being the South of England Oyster Company, with Captain John Woods as managing director, and James Dilnott as the local manager.

In the 1840s the fishermen of Hayling were engaged in oyster dredging to a great extent, clearing land on which to store young oysters in order that they might grow and fatten. This is where they ran foul of the Lord of the Manor, William Padwick, who claimed his right to the soil, and brought several court actions for trespass against the fishermen. This was just one of the storms they had to weather through the years; probably their greatest problem, and one that is still with us, was that of pollution. Drainage schemes for Hayling were put forward with alarming regularity in the early part of this century, feelings being at their strongest in the 1920s when a scheme costing £26,000 was presented. A group of local fishermen led by Mr. Moore protested that the fishing would be polluted, pointing out that if the effluent was discharged at flood-tide it would flow rapidly up the harbour, thus affecting the oyster dredging. As it happened, it did not really matter, for by the 1930s many of the best oyster beds had been reclaimed, with one being used for tennis courts, and another converted into a swimming pool for a local holiday camp. Of course, there were other fish in the sea, and the local fishermen earnt their crust from the wide variety of fish to be found in the adjacent harbours, including fine quality prawns and a small but delicious species of mackerel known as "Hayling Bay Mackerel".

Working on a farm seems to have contributed towards a long

Waterworks Corner, Havant Road, c. 1907

South Hayling – Queen Victoria's "Diamond Jubilee" Fountain on Grand Hotel Corner, Beach Road

and healthy life, for in the obituary news of the local papers the farmworkers who passed on always appeared to have reached a ripe old age. Francis Spittles, for example, died in 1947 at the age of 83, having spent over fifty years of his working life as a shepherd on Hayling Island, being employed by Mr. Twine in his early days, then by Mr. Turner, both of these gentlemen being well known local farmers. But Francis had a long way to go to beat the record of Edmund Bettesworth, for when he died in 1938 he was one hundred years old. Edmund had also worked as a shepherd, and as a youth he tended a flock of 200 sheep that grazed on the Beachlands, a site that was later to be made into a car park. He was also called upon to carry out other farm chores, especially at harvest time. Of course in those days there was no sophisticated machinery to assist in harvesting and the corn was cut, tied in sheaves, and stacked by hand. Edmund had to deliver the hay also, sometimes as far as Portsmouth and this he did by horse wagon using the Langstone Wadeway at low tide to cross to the mainland.

Without the aid of machinery, the farmers of days gone by had a much closer relationship with their animals, especially their faithful old horses. With this in mind, one can imagine the feelings of farmer Richard Roberts of Ham Farm in the last century when he lost his four-legged friend, the poor beast dying under most unusual circumstances. The horse grazed in a field that backed on to the house of Mr. Clinker the well-known South Hayling wheelwright, who was also an ardent beekeeper and kept islanders well supplied with honey. One July day in 1884 Mr. Clinker's bees swarmed from a hive and flew into Mr. Robert's field, Mr. Clinker took a hive into the field and left it there for the rogue bees to return to, and sure enough they did. But unfortunately, as the horse was moving around the field he put his hoof on the hive and overturned it. The bees immediately attacked the animal, causing it to jump over Mr. Clinker's garden hedge in order to escape their fury, but as it landed it mowed down fourteen other hives, and subsequently fell victim to even more bees. The poor old horse was found later, dead in a ditch, there was hardly a part of its body that had not been stung.

As the last of those wonderful wind-driven objects of affection disappeared from the Hayling landscape in 1890, I think I am safe in assuming that there is no one who can recall seeing a windmill on the Island. The North Hayling windmill suffered the fate of so many of its kind, ravaged by fire, the last owner being Mr. George Sparkes. Throughout its history, Hayling could boast at least two other windmills, hence the area that has always been known as Windmill Hill. This mill and others have been covered very comprehensively in another book in the "Down Memory Lane" series, *The Windmills of Hampshire* by Anthony Triggs.

Moving from wind to water power, readers will not recall the old Hayling Tide Mill that flourished into the last century. This mill, which was situated on the eastern shore opposite the Maypole Inn, was indeed an ancient structure, for in the reign of Edward the First in 1294 it was written that the mill was taken with the Manor from the Abbey of St. Peter's of Jumieges by the Crown, valued at that time at sixty shillings. As the tide water rose it over-spilled into a feeding pond that was controlled by flood-gates, this allowed a large water-wheel to be rotated by the waters ebb. During the last century the mill became delapidated, and it was restored to good working order in 1876, the work including the provision of a new water-wheel. This turned out to be a waste of time and money, for sadly the mill was completely destroyed by fire on 5 January, 1877.

The combination of a mild climate with steady rainfall, and a good soil of heavy brick loam makes it easy to grow most types of vegetables and crops as well as supporting beef and dairy cattle, poultry and sheep. The many small farms on Hayling have not changed much over the last fifty years, nor have their choice of

Tournerbury Lane

Station Road, West Town in quieter days

Northney Village

Thatched splendour in Northney

Elm Grove Free Church

crops, according to several local farmers, but their production and efficiency have increased. The largest farm is Manor Farm where there is a rotation of cows, grass and crops as various as wheat, barley, french beans for freezing and peas which are sent to Baxters for canning. Potatoes, onions and cauliflower are also grown and sold mainly in the Portsmouth area. The farm's herd of cows provide milk for the island. A few years ago this farm pioneered the growing of a crop of beans used for making baked beans. The crop was successful but the costs were still greater than importing American-grown beans, so the idea was abandoned.

A natural hazard for Hayling farmers have been the Russian migrant Brent Geese, which in recent years since the legal protection of these birds, have built up in numbers to far exceed the availability of natural food supplied from the harbour, so they have been finishing their meals in the farmers' fields. In particular they graze on the winter wheat, and the birds have become so tame they are difficult to frighten away.

Stoke fruit farm, the well known fruit and vegetable growers was started after World War I by N.M. Wilson, who opened the farm's retail shops in 1927. The farm was taken over by R.A. Wilson after the last war and a third generation, Simon Wilson, is in charge today. Fruit farming is a fairly recent venture but people come from miles around for the luscious strawberries in the summer.

As already mentioned, the oyster dredging in Langstone Harbour received a setback amongst the individual oyster bed owners during the mid 1800s when Padwick was Lord of the Manor of Hayling. Oyster dredgers from Colchester, Portsmouth etc. helped themselves to the beds at the beginning of each season up until 1868, when the particularly delicious Hayling species suddenly became scarce. About that time experiments in France led scientists to believe that oysters could be bred artificially and in 1865 the South of England Oyster Company managed by J. Dilnot, was formed, farming mainly to the west of Hayling. By 1890 they were the best beds in England. The company operating at present is the Langstone Oyster Company at North Hayling Holt, licensed by Havant Borough Council. The eroded walls that surrounded the two beds have been rebuilt and the delicacies produced are marketed in Portsmouth.

"Oh I Do Like To Be Beside The Seaside"

With modern communications being what they are, the train, improved road systems, and the family motor-car, I would not think that there are many youngsters growing up today who will be able to say that they never saw the sea throughout their lifetime, but for those living inland this was quite a common statement in years gone by. Imagine being penned in by town and city walls until your dying day, never able to sample the delights of strolling along a sandy shore, nor watch the sea shimmer and sparkle under a golden sun, nor fill the lungs with intoxicating fresh air. No wonder consumption was rife up until the early days of this century.

The health-giving properties of sea water and ozone were not generally realised until the 18th Century, when little fishing villages throughout the country were transformed into seaside spas overnight, one of the more notable being Brighton on the Sussex coastline. With the patronage of George the Fourth, its rise to fame was spectacular to say the least. The 18th Century may have been the age of the spa, but the 19th was the age of the seaside resort, for with the coming of the railways, excursions to the coast were brought within the reach of many. Victorian entrepreneurs were not slow to realise the prosperity that could be enjoyed by coastal resorts that attracted visitors, and

Not a swimming costume in sight. Hayling beach c. 1903

The Royal Hotel in the early 1900s

The Royal Hotel in the early 1800s

Beachlands and Bus Station, late 1930s

Sea Front Café, the Old Bath House, now demolished

proceeded to build architectural palaces for the purpose of pleasure and profit.

Hayling actually attracted the attention of promoters before young Victoria sat upon her throne, one in particular, Sir Richard Hotham the founder of Bognor, had aspirations to convert the Island into a resort that would rate as one of the finest on the South Coast. Unfortunately, Sir Richard's enthusiasm cooled and the running was left for others to take up, particularly the aforementioned Duke of Norfolk, Sir George Staunton, William Padwick, and other Hayling enthusiasts. They began their ambitious scheme by building a bridge, as mentioned in a previous section, the structure being officially opened in 1824. Immediately a number of palatial villas began to appear including Norfolk Crescent, Stamford Lodge, Richmond House, Staunton House and Stamford House. Clarke's Guide described the buildings as "excellent houses with enclosed grounds belonging to resident gentlemen", whilst its adjectives for properties in the lower bracket took the form of "detached ornamental cottages with prettily arranged gardens that are well stocked with wall fruits, shrubs and flowers".

To cater for holiday makers, the Royal Hotel was built on the beach near Richmond House. An interesting story is associated with the erection of this hotel, for whilst the foundations were being laid in December 1825, workmen found two human skeletons. The *Hampshire Telegraph* of that date went to great lengths to inform its readers that the bones were in very good condition, well preserved, and found some four feet below the surface. One set of remains was just buried in the bare earth, but the other inside a neat coffin, with a date on the lid, 1707.

Described in the early guide books as being an excellent and commodious building, the Royal Hotel must indeed have presented a splendid addition to the Hayling water-front, and provided for its patrons unrivalled views across the Solent to the Isle of Wight. In addition to the hotel facilities, for gentlemen with sporting tastes the Royal boasted a large Billiard Room, where gentlemen could while away an hour or so whilst the ladies retired to the lounge. Of course, if the weather was behaving itself, what better than a pleasant stroll across the lush turf that lay 'twixt beach and hotel. Close to the beach and on a line with the hotel, stood the Library, a classic building with pillars and a pediment in the Ionic style, suggesting to the beholder the appearance of a temple. Once inside, the visitor had access to a varied choice of literature, plus a selection of periodicals and newspapers that allowed one to keep abreast of world events. The building also included a picture gallery and a separate room where chess could be played. From this, one may conclude that holidaymaking in the last century was carried out in a vastly different manner than it is today, in which a game of bingo, hamburgers smothered in onions, and a fast ride on the Wild Mouse, may be considered by many to be the highlight of their hols!

Before we start debating what the Victorians would have thought of "Kiss-me-Quick" hats, we will move along the beach in an easterly direction, and there, but a couple of hundred yards away we would have found the Bath House. Depending on taste and physical resilience, within this building one could partake of a hot, tepid, or cold bath. But just outside bathing machines were available for the more hardy of the human species, those who preferred the invigorating delights of sea bathing. In later years when bathing in the sea became more popular with the masses, the old Bath House was converted into a cafe. The once resplendent Library was also used for this purpose at one time, until it attracted the attention of the demolition hammer in 1936. To complete our mini-tour of some of Hayling's early resort attractions, a must on the visitor's itinery would have been a stroll around the Nursery Gardens, where a wide variety of plants

The vital link, around the time of the opening

Pre-war view of Hayling Bridge

Langstone, the other side of the Bridge

Langstone Mill, c. 1905

flourished in the Island's relatively mild climate. There was also a large hothouse and conservatory in the gardens in which exotic blooms were exhibited.

Another who realised the health giving properties of Hayling sunshine was a gentleman called Treloar who was Lord Mayor of London one year. He founded a charity in order to build hospitals to help the poor from the slums. In Hampshire Mr. Treloar established two children's hospitals, one in Alton and one at Sandy Point. It was discovered that the sun's rays had curative effects for T.B. sufferers, the morning sun was meant to be particularly good, and Hayling sun was stronger than elsewhere along the coast. The Sandy Point hospital had sun beds laid out in the grounds for the young patients which could be seen by yachtsmen sailing past. Rolls-Royce ambulances transported the children from London to Alton and Hayling. When the National Health reorganisation took place his hospital was converted to cater for handicapped and retarded children.

This eastern end of the Island was fairly wild until this century. Land was gradually sold off as building plots along Southwood Road, purchasers often using disused railway carriages as accommodation on their plot. The land could be bought quite cheaply from the farmers, and the private railway companies used to sell off their old carriages inexpensively. This led to a haphazard development at the eastern end but now most of those quaint carriages have gone, being demolished to make way for brick dwellings. Dr. Wright organised much of the development in the Bracklesham Road area. The new estate there was developed by him after 1930. The area was properly laid out with wide roads and typical seaside homes with the living rooms upstairs. By 1935 the population of Hayling was about 5,000.

The Vital Link

There is little doubt that the new found interest in Hayling Island as a desirable place in which to reside or take one's holiday, was influenced a great deal by the improved access afforded by the bridge, the opening of which was indeed a momentous occasion in the Island's history.

Let us go back to that great day in September 1824, a large crowd was assembled at the new bridge, the air was buzzing with excitement as the arrival of the dignitaries was awaited. Earlier in the day the Duke of Norfolk had landed on the mainland from his magnificent yacht, boarding his carriage and four he left with the main party from Havant, with Sir George Staunton and William Padwick leading the way on horseback. Along the way, the leadership of this cavalcade was taken over by two men carrying the King's Colours, and the band of the Royal Marines, Portsmouth Division.

The crowd cheered as the impressive line-up of officials and escorts approached the bridge at noon, as they crossed in order to reach the Hayling side, it was estimated that at one time there was something in the region of one hundred carriages assembled on the bridge. The Duke and his supporters stayed a short while on the good earth of Hayling, then returned to Mr. Padwick's house at Warblington for further celebrations. The ale flowed like water, and those who were still standing by the end of the afternoon were invited to partake of a splendid meal. The dinner, provided by Mr. Holdaway of the Bear Inn at Havant, was much appreciated, and provided an excuse for even more toasts. Meanwhile, back at the bridge large crowds were still gathered to gaze in wonder at this magnificent structure, whilst they listened to lively music being played by a band on board a steam vessel belonging to the Portsmouth and Arundel Navigation Company. Yes, that was quite a day!

Eastoke Corner, Southwood Road

The Old Station Stores, West Town

A leafy Manor Road

Creek Road, Eastoke in the 1930s

Mention of the above company reminds us of that ill-fated venture known as the Portsmouth and Arundel Canal, first mooted in 1815. The idea was to construct a waterway between Arundel and Portsmouth. Encouraged by prophesies that half the sea trade of London would pass along it, work began in 1818 with the first spade being put into the ground at the Ford end by Mr. J. Williams, the chief projector of the enterprise. To allow water access for the canal boats between Langstone and Hayling, a cut was dredged to cut across the Wadeway. The canal entered Portsea Island from Langstone Harbour, and ran to a basin that was sited in the area we now know as Arundel Street. The entire length of the canal was opened for traffic on 26 May 1823, a procession of boats sailing from Arundel passed through the Portsmouth and Hayling end on the following day, the spectacle being witnessed by some 20,000 people. So, when the Hayling bridge was opened in September of the following year, it was amidst a great degree of optimism relating to the benefits that the presence of a thriving canal might bring. Unfortunately, the canal was a failure besieged by troubles throughout its relatively short history. The company was eventually wound up and the canal route in Portsmouth was filled in and converted to a road, of which Goldsmith Avenue forms a large stretch.

Hayling Bridge has had a happier history although in the first fifty years of this century it appeared that the subject of removing the toll charge from the bridge was brought up at every council meeting. Feelings were at their strongest in the 1920s and 30s, the tolls being described as a relic of antiquity by many Island folk who claimed that free access would produce more visitors. No doubt this line of thought was strongly supported by the local shopkeepers and tradesmen, but it brought opposition from other residents who believed the presence of more visitors would spoil their peace and tranquility.

Even in the late Thirties the tollbridge fee was 8d for a car. It became well known for young people returning to the Island late at night to ensure that they returned after midnight – the time the tollkeeper went home and passage over the bridge was for free. If a car arrived just before midnight, it was not unknown to hide round the corner until that hour had passed. It saved 8d, and when one considers that the average craftsman earnt 1/2d per hour it was worthwhile. Many years were to pass before the toll was removed, the last ticket being purchased by the Chairman of Hampshire County Council, Mr. Alan Lubbock, on 11 April, 1960. The removal of the toll charge was good news for motorists, but not so good for flag-sellers, for they did very well by making their way along the long waiting lines of cars that accumulated on the bridge during the weekend and holiday periods, the poor old motorists being sitting prey. Of course, from that date the tollkeeper was made redundant, Mr. Scutt and Mr. Bastin being the last collectors, being preceded by a list that included Albert Budd, George Stanford, Mr. Gooden and the Little Family.

Eventually the Old Hayling Bridge was replaced by a modern concrete structure. This historic event took place in 1956 when the new bridge was opened amidst pomp and ceremony, but the celebrations really paled by comparison with the original bridge opening of 1824. Maybe because by 1956 the price of ale had risen sharply from its original halfpenny a pint!

Roads, Rails, and Ferries

The original 1820s plans of making Hayling into a super coastal resort never really got off the ground. Many of the building projects were not completed, and subsequently abandoned. Despite this, the fight to attract visitors and new residents went on. In this battle it became obvious that new and improved systems of communication were required desperately.

The roads of Hayling gradually evolved from old cart tracks, so they are therefore very winding with a good many bends to negotiate. Although some improvements have been attempted through the years, notably at the school and waterworks bends, Hayling in the 1980s still demands a fair degree of wheel-turning on the part of the motorist. But I am not really being critical, for I feel that this adds to the charm of the Island, and after all, once one leaves Hayling there are enough stretches of motorway to satisfy even the keenest motorist.

Without the volume of traffic, the Hayling roads of yesteryear did not really present a problem, the warning sounds of horses clip-clopping through the quiet lanes could be heard some distance away. In the first half of this century horse-drawn coaches still ruled the highways. As far as Islanders were concerned, the problem was getting to Havant, once there the world was their oyster, for coaches could be caught by the adventurous traveller for such exotic climes as Portsmouth, Brighton, Southampton, or London. The coach services flourished under the names of the Independent Coach, or the Defiance Coach. One service was known as the Queen Coach, operated by Messrs. Faulkner; this was one of the first coach services to include a stop at Hayling.

The Queen Coach could be boarded at the Royal Hotel every morning at 9 o'clock, except Sundays, it then proceeded via Havant, Bedhampton, and Cosham. Alighting at the Fountain Hotel in Portsmouth High Street, one could either spend the day in Pompey, returning to Hayling in the late afternoon, or catch the famous Rocket Coach to London, the ultimate terminal being the Gloucester Coffee House in Piccadilly. The coach fare from Hayling to London was 24 shillings for a seat inside the coach, or the more hardy traveller could sit outside for only fourteen shillings!

Prior to the coming of the railway to Hayling, a service of horse-buses operated to link the Island with Havant. Simon Bone was a well known driver on this service, and could be found sitting up front in all weathers, reminding us that if road travel was tough on passengers at times, it was even tougher for the drivers of these vehicles. Simon Bone was assisted by his young son John, who officially worked on the buses as a conductor-boy. Unfortunately, John Bone lost a leg when he was a teenager, and on leaving the horse-buses he went to work at the Royal Shades public house in South Hayling, where he stayed for over thirty years. Despite the fact that he only had one leg, John was a fine swimmer, and in his unofficial capacity as a lifeguard he did in fact save many lives during the bathing season. He obviously had a strong constitution for he was 85 years old when he died in 1938.

I expect many islanders miss their very own railway, known as the Hayling Billy. My immediate thoughts go back to a hot summer day in the early 50s, I had boarded the Hayling Branch train at Havant and was sitting in a carriage with my thoughts on reaching that sandy beach and shimmering briny as soon as possible. As the train departure time came, there was a slight movement up ahead and a puff of steam passed the window. Then everything became deadly quiet and still, the Hayling Billy had steamed off into the blue and left the carriage standing in the station! Evidently, this was quite a common occurrence for half the train to be left behind, hence regular passengers ensuring that they got a carriage as near the engine as possible!

Let us go back to the beginning of Hayling's railway era. On its line through to Portsmouth, the London Brighton & South Coast Railway arrived at Havant in 1847. This was good news for Havant, and the town had even more to celebrate in 1859 with the arrival of the London & South Western line from Waterloo, despite a good deal of protesting from the Brighton railway company. This development was viewed with great interest by

Langstone Halt

South Hayling Station c. 1905. Pigeons awaiting flying instructions. Courtesy: Lens of Sutton

South Hayling Station Courtesy: Lens of Sutton

Terrier No. 32646 at South Hayling Courtesy: Lens of Sutton

The Puffing Billy waiting to leave Havant Station
Courtesy: Lens of Sutton

Arrival of No. 32650 at South Hayling
Courtesy: Lens of Sutton

Horse-taxi days at Hayling *Courtesy: Lens of Sutton*

Langstone Halt *Courtesy: Lens of Sutton*

No. 2655 steaming out of Havant *Courtesy: Lens of Sutton*

North Hayling Halt *Courtesy: Lens of Sutton*

those who were dedicated to promoting Hayling, such a valued link but a "stone's throw" away from the Island was an opportunity not to be missed, so plans were made to construct a railway line to link Hayling with Havant, and subsequently the rest of the country. Neither the L.S.W.R. nor the L.B.S.C.R. was interested in providing a line to Hayling Island, so a private firm the Hayling Railway Company was formed.

Incorporated by an Act of Parliament in 1860, the company was given the task of raising something in the region of £66,000 for the project, seven years being the deadline for completion. As per usual in railway line construction, many problems became apparent in the next few years, both physically and financially. Although a line to Langstone had been completed by 1865, and was providing a valuable service by transporting various goods from the quay, including coal, corn and gravel, things looked bleak for the completion of the Hayling section. It was at this point that the day was saved by Mr. Francis Fuller, a wealthy estate agent from London, who became interested in promoting Hayling as a prosperous resort. Fuller proceeded to induce financial aid and a renewed enthusiasm for the Island's future, and the railway project was given a much-needed boost through his assistance.

Renewed effort was put into the construction of the line, and a wooden bridge gradually appeared to traverse the channel between Langstone and Hayling, a continuing line through to South Hayling soon following. At last it was completed, and on 28 June 1867 the first train arrived on the Island. That day was remembered fondly by our old centenarian friend Edmund Bettesworth, who, in between shepherding his sheep had actually been employed in the construction of the railway line. However, due to a number of construction faults, the line did not actually open for passenger service until 17 July. But, after the seven-year long battle, what did the difference of another couple of weeks wait make? Hayling had gained a much needed railway system.

Although most of the rail visitors to Hayling were drawn to the beaches in the southern part of the isle, if the railway line had run from Havant to South Hayling Station only, it would not have served much purpose for those living in the northern extremes. So, for their convenience there were two halts situated along the route, one being at Langstone, the other at North Hayling. These intermediate stops did not have any railway staff in attendance, passengers purchasing their tickets from the guard. All in all, it was a very friendly service, with the train waiting for anyone who was remotely near the halt: all the intending passenger had to do was wave a hand.

In those far-off days before the turn of the century, the Hayling railway was popular for school trips from Havant and the surrounding area, and became affectionately known as the "Crab and Winkle" line. Many youngsters formed friendships with the driver and his guard, driver Neddy Rag was only too happy to show them around his cab, and guard Bob Outen let them wave his coveted flag.

Through the years many plans were put forward to link Hayling Island with Southsea; first it was proposed that it should be a rail link, and in later years ideas of using trams were regularly muted. Such schemes were almost realized in 1886, when a plan to link the two resorts was proposed by a private company. It was to be named the Portsmouth & Hayling Railway, and would join the existing Hayling line just above the starting signal at South Hayling Station. From this point the line would bend sharply to run behind Poplar Cottages, then proceed across mudland to the south of Norfolk Lodge until it reached the mouth of Langstone Harbour. The line was to cross the harbour by means of a eight-span viaduct with a swing bridge, the total length being some 900ft. It was to provide for both rail and road traffic, and to also provide a footway for pedestrians. On the Portsmouth side the route would run close to the Thatched House public house, along the side of the canal, and eventually into Fratton Station. On the Hayling side it was also proposed to build a wharf on the foreshore, by the side of the shooting butts, and a siding to be laid to connect with the main line of the link. The plans for this four mile long rail link were displayed for public inspection at the house of the Parish Clerk, Mr. Bowers. It all came to nothing though and another ambitious plan fell flat.

Mention of a swing bridge reminds me of the bridge that carried the single line on the northern approach to the Island, officially known as the Langstone Harbour Swing Bridge. The opening over the waterway allowed a span of 30 feet for vessels to pass through, the girders of the opening portion being pivoted by a wrought iron cylinder travelling on a roller path, the wheel gathering being worked by hand. In this book the reader will discover a rare photograph of the swing bridge in the opening position, with a vessel passing through.

The Hayling line was taken over by the L.B.S.C.R., and was operated by the company until 1 January, 1923, this being the date the Southern Railway absorbed the line into its network. Under Southern steam the line jogged along merrily enough through the pre-war years, with only the odd grumble here or there. One of the latter occurred in 1925, the complaint coming from Hayling residents who felt that their social life was considerably handicapped by the fact that the railway company did not allow for a late train back to Hayling from Portsmouth, and theatre-goers were unable to stay and enjoy a play through to the end. This was frightfully inconvenient, especially in the case of thrillers and who-dunnit's. Southern Railway lent a sympathetic ear and brought into service a late train on one night of the week, thus making Wednesday night the time for Hayling theatre fiends to plan their night-out. There was another outcry in 1930 when rumours circulated around the Island that for economic reasons the railway company was going to close the Hayling branch line for the winter months. The South Hayling Parish Council were alarmed at this news, declaring that such a move would set Hayling back at least fifty years, but their fears were groundless.

The line received a boost in the 1930s, as new generations of holidaymakers began to discover the delights of Hayling, helped by the fact that a faster service was provided when the Waterloo and Brighton routes via Havant were electrified. Then along came the war, and everyone had to pack away their buckets and spades for six years or so. The Hayling railway did its bit for the war effort, ferrying back and forth the many Servicemen who were stationed in the area.

During the second world war the War Office had a 'plane sent up to take aerial photographs of Portsmouth at night to show the main lighting system. The lights on Hayling were then organised in a similar pattern and when the air raid sirens went up the lights in Portsmouth went out and the Hayling lights went on. The deception worked on at least two occasions, and protected the heavily populated Portsea Island.

After the war, British folk came out of the gloom and descended upon the coast once more, determined to enjoy themselves, and who could blame them? Holiday camps fell in with this spirit, with the Hayling camps attracting many thousands each summer, and of course, the Hayling railway enjoyed brisk business. However, an enemy was on the horizon – the family motor car. Gradually more and more branch lines were axed, and the end of the Island's railway era was drawing near.

Despite objections from residents and local authorities, the last run was made on 3 November, 1963, with enthusiasts

Vessel passing through Langstone Swing Bridge, 1913

The Hayling Ferry and Pontoon

Arrival of the Ferry at Hayling Pontoon

The Ferryboat Sinah

Early motoring days on Hayling. Bert Lawrence in his new £100 Ford 'T'

invading the area in their thousands to witness this historic moment in railway history. But memories fade, before long the tracks became choked with weeds, those same tracks that had carried countless numbers of happy faces to sample Hayling's balmy breezes, and gain a welcome break from the confines of the city. In an effort to keep fond memories alive, a public house was opened sporting the name "Hayling Billy", and one of these beloved engines was displayed in the car park as a permanent memorial to the line. Unfortunately for Hayling, this engine was removed in 1979 for restoration work, following which it resumed its working life in 1981 over on the Isle of Wight. Although it was the loss of a tourist attraction as far as Hayling was concerned, it is a pleasant thought that a "Hayling Billy" is still providing enjoyment for holidaymakers.

The other major form of transport was the Hayling Ferry, that valued service that links the south-western tip of Hayling to Southsea. In operation for a good many years, it is impossible to estimate the vast number of travellers who used this service, not only to commute to their work in Portsmouth, but also to escape from the stony beach of Southsea to the sandy shores of Hayling.

The name that features synonymously with the ferry is that of Spraggs, for this family operated the crossing for many years, and were also proprietors of the Norfolk Inn at the mouth of the harbour. The current at this point has always been exceedingly treacherous, and has claimed many lives over the years. In April 1922 these waters brought about the death of the ferry proprietor, George Spraggs, who was drowned in front of his own house. The incident occurred when his two sons, George and Cyril, were mooring a boat on the pontoon, the sea was extremely rough at the time, causing young George to fall into the water. He was carried under the pontoon, Cyril moved to the other side and attempted to pull him out, holding on like grim death Cyril called for help. His father reacted immediately, but as he stepped on to the pontoon he slipped into the water himself, within seconds he disappeared from sight. George was rescued, and the ferry services continued under the name of the Spraggs Brothers.

Not all the accidents at the harbour mouth ended in tragedy, for many people were lucky enough to escape with only a severe soaking, and very often it was the Spraggs ferry boat that effected their rescue. In just one such incident in the 1930s, a man fell over the side of a motorboat and was soon in great difficulty. A young lady dived in to save him, and although she was a strong swimmer, the current got the best of her also. The incident was seen by Mr. Gomer and Mr. Eatwell in the Spraggs boat, who quickly sped to the spot, they managed to pull the lady out first, then they turned their attention to the man, successfully rescuing him also. So, thanks to their quick thinking, two lives were saved that day.

In the following years questions of financial viability came to the fore, and eventually Portsmouth City Council ran the ferry service. Members of the Transport Committee were not happy with the situation and its Chairman declared that the Hayling Ferry was a burden on the Portsmouth ratepayers, so the ferry made its last crossing under this support on 31 March 1981. Following this, Mr. C. Edwards and Mr. M. Dutfield commenced a private service which was subsidized by Hampshire County Council in its first year. Subsidies were approved for a further three years. Let us hope that this vital link across Langstone Harbour is retained, not only for the convenience of the public, but also because it is part of the Island's history.

For Those In Peril On The Sea

Recalling the flag-sellers on Hayling Toll Bridge, it is fairly certain that one of the good causes that those smiling ladies rattled their collecting boxes for was the Royal Life-boat Fund. Back in the old days the crew were not fortunate enough to possess the sophisticated equipment that is available to modern life-boat stations and vessels, it was very much a case of "man against the elements", and called for a very special breed of men. For nearly sixty years Hayling was able to call upon a number of her sons who were willing to sacrifice life and limb in order to save the lives of others.

The Hayling life-boat story began in January 1865, the schooner Ocean was being severely battered by an extremely ferocious storm. The ship was powerless against the huge waves that hurled it on to the bar at the entrance to Langstone Harbour, where it began to break up rapidly. The plight of the crew was seen by Major Festing of the Royal Marine Artillery, who was a resident of Hayling. Without hesitation he gathered a group of local fisherman to crew a boat belonging to Fort Cumberland, then displaying great bravery this gallant band set off for the wrecked vessel. Overcoming fantastic odds they managed to save all but two of the Ocean's crew, and thankfully returned to Hayling to tell the tale.

This incident made apparent the vital need for a life-boat on this part of the coast, where the rocks known as the Woolsinors presented a constant peril. Major Festing enlisted the aid of Mr. G. Sandeman and the Rev. C. Hardy to campaign for a permanent life-boat, the sum of £550 being the amount required to realize this project. They had no need to worry however, for Messrs. Leaf & Son of Old Change in the City of London generously donated the whole amount. The old life-boat station is now the Beach Cote Cafe on the seafront near the golf course.

The nearby Seaview Terrace which had been built in 1825 by the Duke of Norfolk as artisans' cottages during the building of the Crescent, was purchased by coastguards in 1865 and re-modelled by them to house the life-boat men who doubled as coastguards, with stables to the rear for the horses which pulled the life-boat to and from the water. This journey eventually became too much and a new lifeboat station was erected at the eastern end of the Island where the boat could be kept nearer to the sea.

Hayling's first lifeboat was launched on 13 September, christened the Olive Leaf. It was indeed a very happy moment in the Island's history. The boat was in fact the most efficient craft of her type in the world at that time, and before being brought to Hayling she was tested for self-righting in London's Regents Park Canal Dock, where the water shipped by her was ejected through patent valves in a time of only 25 seconds. With the Bishop of Chichester on hand to bless her at the launching, the 32ft. long by 7 ft. wide Olive Leaf presented a magnificent sight as she was pulled into the sea for the first time, and deserved the hearty cheering that resounded on the beach that day.

During her 23 years of service the Olive Leaf was launched for rescue purposes nine times, and to her credit was responsible for the saving of 32 lives. She was replaced by the Charlie and Adrian lifeboat in 1888, which in turn was replaced by the Proctor in 1914. That particular year was one that the Hayling lifeboat service would like to have forgotten, it was also the year that Lt. Basil Hall was appointed as the Inspector for Lifeboats on the South Coast, so he visited Hayling to inspect the new boathouse. To show their prowess, the Charlie and Adrian was launched, and the crew under coxswain George Miller went through their exercises. It turned out to be a chapter of disasters from the word go, the first being when Coastguardman Cowell set off the signal rocket for he took too long over the fuse and the rocket went off with his hand over it. But, carrying on regardless, the new boathouse doors were flung open to launch the life-boat. Regrettably, a slight miscalculation was made with

Launching of the Olive Leaf Lifeboat, 1865

Charlie and Adrian Lifeboat, c. 1906

Sea View Terrace, Mr. Barber's Bakery on right

Launching of Proctor, 1914

The new Life boat House and Coastguard Cottages around 1910

regard to the height of the boathouse door, as the rudder of the boat was badly damaged as it passed through, and was completely useless by the time that the craft had entered the water. This resulted in the life-boat floundering around in all directions, with the crew desperately attempting to steer it with their oars! The chief members of the Life-boat Committee, Commander Oliver and Lt. Allen, could only look on in utter dismay!

Throughout its existence the Hayling life-boat service could boast an excellent array of hard-working coxswains, this list including William Goldring, Sam Goldring, John Goldring, George Miller, and Charles Cole. Crewing his first life-boat at the age of 18, Charles Cole took over as coxswain in 1919, and was in fact the last to hold this office, his brother Ernie acted as second coxswain.

Despite a great deal of protesting, the Hayling Life-boat Station was closed on 29 September, 1924, made redundant by the introduction of two motor lifeboats installed at Bembridge and Selsey. A crew led by Charles Cole sailed the Proctor over to Cowes, where she was overhauled before going to Berwick-on-Tweed to continue her good work. She seemed to know that she was bidding farewell to Hayling, and according to the crew she sailed like a dream on that last journey, reaching Ryde in under the hour. It was a sad moment as she left the Hayling shore for the last time, tears fell unabashed, and George Jones, who gave 28 years of his life to the lifeboat service, summed it up for everyone when he said: "It is like losing an old friend".

Another link with the sea was lost in 1933 when the Coastguard Cottages, which had formed part of the Coastguard Station, situated behind the new boathouse, were put up for auction under the hammer of Messrs. King & King. The nine cottages and a plot of building land were sold for a total of £3,280.

Finally, mention of the coastguards reminds me of a story that took place in 1805; a vessel was driven on to the Poles opposite Eastoke, and was in dire trouble. But it was discovered that the plague had broken out on board the boat, and the coastguard was given instructions to shoot the first person who attempted to reach the shore. However, some compassion was shown by the authorities, and fresh food was passed along a rope for the passengers and crew. Unfortunately, the storm blew up again, even worse than before, and the vessel broke up with all on board perishing.

Toads and Loch Ness Monsters

In 1875, the magazine *Land and Water* printed a letter from one of its readers about an unusual experience which occurred whilst he was on holiday at Hayling Island. Evidently the chap in question was bathing one morning from the beach, when he saw a large toad, quite the biggest that he had ever seen. The toad entered the water and started heading out to sea, so the bather followed it out as far as he dare. When the man turned back for shore, the toad was some 300 yards out and going strong towards the Nab Light.

The writer was quite amazed at the toad's behaviour, but when he recounted his tale to a local fisherman, he learnt something even more astonishing. The fisherman could remember an incident that took place fifty years before, in 1825; evidently that particular season was exceedingly dry, and drought conditions prevailed. This prompted all the toads on Hayling Island to take to the sea; according to the old fisherman this produced amazing scenes on the Island's beaches, with toads bouncing all over the place in order to get to the water.

But this was not as strange as the experience encountered by a boat filled with Emsworth fishermen in 1934. The chaps were fishing quite peacefully, when suddenly a great monster loomed out of the water. It was awful, large head, huge brown eyes, a long pointed snout, and the body of a gigantic eel. Of course, after they had got back and told their tale of the sighting, nobody would believe them, the affair not being helped by the fact that the incident took place on April the First!

Our monster tale did not end there, for a week later a strange monster was washed on to the beach by the Hayling Sailing Club at Salterns. The remains of the unusual creature were in an advanced state of decomposition, the movement of the waves must have performed in such a way to make the fishermen who first saw it think that it was still alive. But, it did indeed have a large head with a pointed snout, and it was estimated that it had some 30 teeth or so. What was it? Nobody had the slightest idea, and it was to remain one of nature's unsolved mysteries.

This was not the first monster washed up on the Hayling shore because a similar incident took place at Eastoke in 1882. The creature was certainly very unusual at first sight, but after much inspection the locals decided that it must have been the remains of a whale carcass. Nobody was more interested in the body of the creature than Mr. Lock, who was better known as "Toby" to the locals. Toby lived on Hayling in a tarred cottage; known as The Black Hut in Mengham Road. He was a travelling tinker of sorts and could be seen driving around the Island with his donkey cart laden down with china, saucepans, brushes, and all manner of hardware supplies. He also bought rags and bones. Yes, that creature certainly caught his attention, and before much time had passed he had removed its flesh and was boiling it down to remove the oil, this process being carried out in a battered pot heating over an open fire. Toby rates as one of Hayling's most colourful and outlandish characters, and when he died in 1918 he was sorely missed, especially by the landlord of the Rose & June where Toby spent most of the profits from his various dealings.

At Your Service

If anyone earnt the title of "Mister Hayling", then it certainly must have been Harry Richard Trigg. Another name to credit this gentleman with might have been "Mister Fixit", for he had his finger in many Hayling pies, and in doing so he played a prominent role in the development of the Island. The directories list Mr. Trigg as a builder, surveyor, auctioneer, coal merchant, and an agent for the Phoenix Insurance Company, but he was involved in many other projects. Despite his various business activities, he managed to find time to produce a really first-class guide book to Hayling.

Hayling had Harry Trigg to thank for introducing gas to the Island, for he established the works that were situated near the Railway Station. The first burner was lit in the August of 1877 by Sir William Humphrey, and the first persons to experience the new wonder were the officers of the Volunteer Camp that encamped at Hayling in the 1870s. The Hayling Gas Company gave good service over the years, with just the occasional moan about the price of it. The biggest outcry was in the 1920s when the company informed the parish council that it intended to charge by the therm instead of by the 1,000 cu. ft., this prompted the council to declare that the price of 1/9d. a therm was highway robbery, and they would fight it through the Board of Trade and go to London if necessary. The big change came in the 1930s, for in 1936 the Hayling Island Gas Company was taken over by the Portsmouth & Gosport Gas Company. In August of 1938 a twelve-inch main was laid from the works at Hilsea, and the manufacturing station at Havant was closed. This event brought instant happiness to Hayling residents, for the price of gas was immediately reduced by 3d.

The wonders of electricity were not introduced on to the Island until the 1920s. It may seem strange now, but in those days towns and villages had to fight to get mains installed. In 1925

Hayling Council School, Sunshine Corner

The Common, Eastoke Corner

A traffic-free Station Road, West Town

Junction of Station Road and West Lane

Beach Road

representation was made to the Portsmouth Corporation Electricity Department as the people of Hayling felt that it was about time that they were able to get "switched-on" like their neighbours in the surrounding areas. In fact, at that time there was a total of 81 houses on the Island that had actually been wired in anticipation of the arrival and availability of electricity. Of course, the mains were eventually installed and the bills followed shortly after.

In the Hayling of yesteryear, the chief complaint appeared to be about drainage, and at almost every council meeting the subject was raised. Even in the 1920s there were many complaints about the bad water supplied at the village pumps, but with the passing of a few years the water supply was improved.

Another vital service was the Post Office, and without the existence of the telephone, in the old days the humble letter played a very important role in daily lives. In the middle of the last century the postal arrangements were in the hands of Mr. James Jenman of South Hayling, and in addition to running the Post Office, James also had his own tailoring business on the same premises at the Seafront. By 1878 the Hayling Post Office was held by George Luff, and incorporated the Telegraph Office and the Savings Bank. As well as being the postmaster, George also had a busy grocery business.

All the Hayling mail had to come and go through the Havant offices, and it was from there that Mr. Fielding operated. He was appointed as postman for Hayling in 1874, and it was his lot in the early days to cover the whole of the Island on foot, but modernization was on its way, and a few years later he was allowed the use of a donkey and cart. Mr. Fielding the friendly postman had problems in 1881, for this was the year of the Great Snowstorm, the blizzard was such that at one stage he was stuck in a drift and only after much difficulty did he manage to claw his way out of it. Imagine his feelings when he struggled to the door of a well known Hayling resident, only to receive a complaint that he was two hours late in delivering the mail! Back in 1928 several Hayling residents brought complaints about the postal service, their gripe being that letters posted at Southampton did not arrive at Hayling until the following morning, and in addition, letters posted from Hayling did not arrive in London on the same day! I wonder what they would have to say about the postal services of today!

Never mind, whilst the worthies of old Hayling were bemoaning the fact that they only had three mail deliveries a day, a new invention was beginning to make its presence known, the telephone. The first telephone exchange on Hayling Island was opened in 1909 by Harry Trigg. To justify opening, the exchange had to have a minimum of eight subscribers, and although Harry had rounded up seven local folk to allow the new talking-wonder into their homes, he had great difficulty finding the eighth customer, but eventually won him over. The first exchange was at Oak Villas in West Lane, but it gradually expanded and a new automatic exchange was opened in 1925. Being able to cater for 300 customers only, this was also made redundant and in turn replaced by a larger exchange erected in Station Road in 1933.

I can remember my old friend Lew Lawrence the Gosport photographer telling me about some of the telephone calls that he made to his relatives at Hayling in the early days of the operator service. Lew was a keen record collector and so he would ring his Hayling cousins, then placing the mouthpiece close to the horn of his wind-up gramophone he would play his latest "top of the pops" favourite. Not only did this go down well in the Lawrence residence at Elm Grove, but also with the Hayling exchange operator who loved to listen in!

In the middle of the last century the school at Hayling was situated in Manor Road, the building being lent rent free by M.

C. Osborn of Fareham. The schoolmaster was Mr. Alfred Miller, who did his best under the circumstances to provide the youngsters with some form of education, but conditions were exceedingly poor in this dark old building, and very Dickensian. Those residents who wanted a better education for their offspring sent them to the Rev. Spurgeon's establishment in Havant, but South Hayling pupils had to walk six miles every morning in order to get to school, and then had the prospect of the walk home at the end of the day.

Having accomplished such a fine job of work in getting Hayling's own lifeboat, that energetic clergyman, the Rev Charles Hardy put his efforts into obtaining a better school and conditions for the youngfolk of the Island. With the help of Mr. Frederick Padwick, who provided a site for the new school, plans went ahead in 1873 and the building was opened a couple of years later, with approximately one hundred pupils. It was a start, and most folk thought that it was £1,500 well spent. A succession of headmasters ruled the school in the first twelve years, gentlemen such as Mr. Gynes and Mr. Watson, but in 1888 the position was taken over by the much respected Mr. A. Logan, who was to remain at the school for 33 years. In Mr. Logan's time the school curriculum was improved tremendously, and I am sure that he will still be remembered by older readers.

When Mr. Logan retired in 1921 his place was taken by Mr. H. Earney who came from Andover to Hayling, the local folk liked him, and he liked the local folk, for he was to remain in this position for 31 years, retiring in 1953. Mr. Earney carried on the good work from 1921, and like his predecessor was responsible for many changes and improvements over the years. The Council School was enlarged in 1934, and the opening ceremony took the form of a double celebration, for it took place on Empire Day. The fun and games included breaking the flag, a display of gymnastics by the pupils, folk dancing, plaiting the Maypole, and much singing. It was a great day for Mr. Earney for he had waited a long while for this expansion work, there being more children than the school could really cope with. The old part of the school was modernised, and the additions included a block of six classrooms, with rooms devoted to science, wood-work, and the basics of cooking. The inventive Mr. Earney also installed a weather station in the school grounds for recording purposes, including the measurement of rainfall. He also did a great deal to encourage sport, cricket being one of his great passions. He was rightly proud of his sports teams who brought the school many successes.

Another service provided for the island this century has been the "Hayling Mosquito Control" Scheme, beginning on 8 April, 1921. J.F. Marshall was the first honorary secretary and provided financial backing. Having a mild climate, mosquitoes had always bred in alarming numbers in the salt marshes and had plagued Islanders for centuries. The Rev. Charles Hardy, who was involved so much with young people and schools, and who died in 1885, used to give children a ½d for every dozen mosquitoes they had killed in order to help cut down the number of flies.

Each female mosquito could lay up to two hundred eggs at a time, but Hardy's efforts were better than none. J.F. Marshall studied the salt marsh mosquitoes under a microscope, then organised the H.M.C. volunteers who worked hard during the Twenties, wiping out the pests by hand by collecting the eggs. Even with the first year of the H.M.C., there were over 150 members who had divided up the Island into 19 sections, each with its own leader. During the next few years, Marshall was in regular contact with the Minister of Health, the Scientific Journal, journalists, schools of medicine, doctors' conferences and universities and the British Museum. He built his laboratory at Seacourt in 1925 and became Founder and Director of the British Mosquito Control Institute and had direct contact with

Westfield House. The Grand Hotel, a convent, now a school

Sea Court, c. 1915

Orchard Lease, now demolished

St. Andrews Suntrap Home, Seafront Road

The Priory, Lynton House School, Victoria Avenue

international mosquito problems. After John Marshall died in 1949, Mr. Staley, with similar qualifications, continued the Hayling mosquito control. He retired in 1958 and his son-in-law continued his work.

Ours Is A Nice House Ours Is

During the 1900s, Hayling began to expand tremendously, this being brought about by a population boom that ultimately led to a building boom. In the preceding years the population figures fluctuated considerably, and reached an all-time low in the 1300s when the Black Death made its presence felt. In 1788, an enterprising curate of Hayling, the Rev. E. Evans, decided to carry out a census of the Island. His figures revealed that in that year the population was 536, this sum comprising 251 males, and 285 females. He also compiled an average list of births, deaths, and marriages for the eight years prior to 1788. The average per year amounted to 19 births, 13 deaths, and six marriages. By this, it would appear that marriage was not a particularly popular institution on Hayling!

By 1911 the Hayling population figures had leapt to 2,280, and by 1921 to 3,300. So, more people, more homes. As the number of folk wishing to sample the delights of the Island increased, so did the invasion of builders. Perhaps, there were too many, for many of these tradesmen appeared in the bankruptcy court. In one such case in 1932, the Registrar was heard to remark that he wondered if Hayling was a resort for holidaymakers, or a retreat for builders, for it was revealed that there were at least 72 builders in business on the Island!

Building competition was keen, so were prices. In 1934 estate agents Pembroke Cross of Hayling were advertising holiday homes by the sea on the Sandy Beach Estate. For the sum of £375 you could be the possessor of a magnificent Suntrap House, complete with three bedrooms, a balcony, and plenty of living space. For the really rich who could afford a little more how about a five-roomed residence for £475? By the way, whether three or five bedroomed, both types of house were detached!

Unfortunately, to make way for housing development and improved road schemes, many fine old residences were demolished in the 20s and 30s. One imposing structure that has survived the attentions of the demolition hammer is the old Westfield House, formerly the home of the renowned Sandeman family. A rather nice plan and original auction details of the Westfield Estate, dated 1870, are on show at Millers Estate Agency offices in Mengham Road.

In the 1880s the property changed hands, and before the turn of the century it was converted into the Grand Hotel, a venture that was doomed to a short existence. It has seen many changes, but I am pleased to observe that the original building still dominates the Seafront, once St. Patrick's convent for many years but now the Choir School of Our Lady and St. John.

Lama House was demolished in the 1930s. An unusual building that possessed a very large tower, it was very popular with seafarers for it was visible from several miles out at sea. It was built by Mr. Trigg for a Mr. Johnson, a gentleman who had extensive interests in Russia. Whilst the building was being demolished, Mr. Snell the contractor found a small bag of coins hidden in the footings. The coins were silver and gold, some English, some Russian. This was quite a remarkable find, for although many house owners often hide momentoes in the foundations whilst a house is being built, after they have left the site the bricklayers generally removed the treasures before they were buried!

Old landmarks were disappearing rapidly by 1935, and in that year West Town Cottage on the corner of West Lane was demolished in order to make way for new shops. This had been the farmhouse of West Town Farm, and although it had been altered through the years it had originally been built on the foundations of a Saxon farmhouse, one of the tithlings into which the Island was divided prior to the Norman Conquest, the others being at Northney, Eastney, Stoke, Westney, and Mengham. Over the years the old cowsheds and stables were demolished to be replaced by shops and houses. Only two years before its demise, the old West Town Cottage had served a very useful purpose, having been taken over by the Social Service Committee and used as a club for the unemployed of Hayling, starting with 30 volunteers being trained to provide a handyman service around the Island, including shoe and boot repairing.

Hollybush Cottage has an interesting history for it was once the home of W.T. Stead the famous journalist and writer. During his period of residence many prominent people were entertained there, including members of the Peerage. Apart from being a staunch member of the Congregational Church on Hayling, Mr. Stead maintained his journalistic interests by producing a small local paper from his home, this was known as the "Hollybush Gazette". It was organised on very professional lines, and contributions had to be received by Wednesday for publication on Friday. Miss Estell Stead acted as Editor, and W.T. himself was the Sub-Editor. Sadly, the great W.T. was to meet his end on the ill-fated maiden voyage of the *Titanic*. A picture of this resplendent gentleman appeared in a special book on the disaster produced by *Lloyds Weekly News*, his last moments were described by a survivor of that dreadful night in 1912. Evidently, as death was about to strike, Stead was standing calmly on the deck whilst other passengers were displaying extreme panic. It was as if he knew what was going to happen. Strangely enough, prior to the *Titanic* disaster Stead had written a tale relating to the perils of icebergs in the Atlantic, and the subsequent fate of liners. A tragic note of prophecy was contained in the words of the story: "The ocean bed beneath the run of the liners is strewn with the whitening bones of thousands who have taken their passages as we have done, but who never saw their destination."

Hollybush Cottage was originally part of a fisherman's cottage. In later years it was altered many times, and during one of these alterations a cleverly concealed smugglers' hiding place was discovered in the chimney stack. Smuggling, by all accounts, was a thriving business in the Hayling of the 18th Century. Hayling provided the base for a most desperate and daring gang of smugglers and cut-throats, the chief of whom was the notorious Gil Brown, who, after a most successful and colourful career was killed in an engagement with one of His Majesty's ships off the Isle of Wight. There is no doubt that this part of the coast lent itself very well to those in the smuggling profession, and they led the authorities a merry chase. The Royal Oak at Langstone was a popular haunt for smugglers, and although the place was watched carefully by coastguards from their old brig the *Griper*, they had little success in catching the law-breakers. For those who would like to know more about local smuggling I would recommend Skelton's 1826 guidebook on Hayling, and Thomas's *The King Holds Hayling*, reprinted 1978 by Pelham of Havant. The latter is the most comprehensive book written about Hayling, and was first published in 1961 by Gordon Thomas, a retired Major. He served on Havant Urban District Council and was concerned with conservation of the history of the island. He was no businessman and so he asked a friend, "Ned" Danby to take care of the business side of the book he was preparing. They raised £1,000 in the form of a loan from local residents in sums of £50 or £100 each, and as they sold the books the money was paid back to the sponsors. The books sold quite readily and all the money was paid back within a year and a half. Three years after his book was published, Major Thomas died in a military hospital in Cardiff.

In addition to Mr. W.T. Stead, another famous writer Neville

Recovering from the excitement of the egg-and-spoon race, 1913

Northney Holiday Camp

An early photograph of Westfield House showing The Grotto now part of the funfair

The Creek and Tournerbury Woods, 1912

Station Road, West Town, 1920s

Shute, chose to live on Hayling Island. Although Shute emerged as one of the world's most renowned authors, he is also remembered in the Portsmouth area for his association with Airspeed Aviation at Portsmouth Airport. It was during this period that he came to live in the beautifully situated Pond Head House in Salterns Lane, and what a marvellous spot for any writer to gaze out on in order to gain inspiration, it certainly worked for Mr. Shute. He was also a reputed fan of the Regal Cinema and although it was not far from his house, used to drive there in his car, using his state petrol allowance.

Pond Head achieved a degree of notoriety in 1984 when it was the scene of a murder. The owner was brutally murdered by the gardener and the event and ensuing trial was the talk of the island.

Victoria Avenue was built to mark Queen Victoria's Jubilee. Local inhabitants were invited to pay £1 to have a horse chestnut tree planted beside the road, with their name and receipt of payment entered in a special register. Three of these registers are known to exist still. Instead of signing their name a few of those paying their £1 had to put a cross as they could not write! The trees were planted pink and white alternately and when they blossom the avenue looks beautiful.

Pound Corner was so named because of the little flint pound which was originally used for impounding stray animals, to prevent them from eating other people's livelihoods. The pound was in existence hundreds of years ago for it was restored in 1778 (the village stocks being removed just a few years before that) and again around 1937. It was Mrs. Clarke, wife of the then Hayling vicar, who had it completely reconstructed with four walls and an oak gate. It stayed like that until the council decided to widen the road and the pound was broken down the middle, so destroying it. It still has part of three walls left and is situated on the inside of the bend, opposite the end of Church Road, now known as "Sunshine Corner".

Leisure And Pleasure

Readers may get the impression from my ramblings into the past that life in days gone by was all work and no play. Certainly they had longer working hours then, but folk still managed to make the best of any free time they may have had. Of course, pleasures were much simpler in the old days. With no television, videos or stereos, entertainment in the home mainly took the form of conversation, music and needlework.

Sport has always played a major part in Island life. Hayling has always been able to boast a number of excellent football and cricket clubs, and although to my knowledge the name of Hayling has not yet been up in lights at Wembley or Lords, a lot of pleasure has been derived from the Island Games through the years. In the 1930s, fun-games of cricket were a regular event, and matches would take place between teams of married and single players. I don't know if it really means anything, but the "Singles" team generally appeared to emerge as the winners. Perhaps the most bizarre games took place between Hayling Men versus Hayling Women, and believe it or not these were always very close matches. Of course, the ladies had a little assistance in that the chaps bowled, batted, and fielded left-handed! The cricket addicts of Hayling had plenty to celebrate in 1935, for in unison with jubilee celebrations of that year a new pavilion was opened at the Staunton Avenue Ground.

The female population of Hayling did not require any help by handicapping when it came to hockey, for the Hayling Island Womens Hockey Club, first formed in 1935, went on from strength to strength, and were dreaded by opposing teams from all over the South. Hayling ladies have also displayed good prowess on the golf course through the years, and that brings us very nicely to the sport for which Hayling has been acclaimed for one hundred years.

We have to thank the Sandeman family of wine and spirit fame for the introduction of golf to the Island, and I must scotch the rumour that they played golf whilst dressed in cloaks and broad-brimmed hats! The head of the family, Colonel John Glas Sandeman, started the ball rolling in 1883, when ground for the course was rented on a long lease from the executors of the Park Estate. Before it was invaded by golfers, the land was the favourite haunt of rabbits, and one could hardly walk more than a couple of steps without falling down a warren. It was also a marvellous venue for poachers, and gamekeepers were employed to keep a sharp look-out, but the crafty poachers generally won the day.

When the Hayling club was formed, golf was little known in the South, and it was at that time one of only ten clubs in the country. Beginning as a private club, its members mostly comprised London and Scottish players. Originally, the first tee was in front of the Royal Hotel, and that building was actually used as the Club House. This was when the course consisted of nine holes in the Beach Common area, but it expanded tremendously even in the first year and they moved west to the old rabbit-infested grounds.

The course gradually developed into one of the finest in the country, and now celebrates its centenary, an attainment of which John Glas Sandeman would have been very proud. Throughout its existence the course has attracted many well-known figures and personalities: Prime Minister James Balfour in 1890, Grand Duke Michael of Russia in 1902, Edward the Seventh, the Prince of Wales (later Edward the Eighth), and his brother the Duke of Kent in addition to many famous golfers who have earnt their place in the record books.

Many epic battles have been played out on the Hayling course, but one match I should like to have seen took place in 1925. It was that year's battle for the Houldsworth Shield, and at the end of the day the Navy champion, the Rev. E. Ulyat, and Dr. Wilfred Harris, were equal with scores of 75. They arranged to settle the matter three days later, but at the 18th hole they had both scored 75 once again. Determined to get a result, they played yet again, but it ended in another tie, 81 each. Exhausted and weary the two players hauled themselves around the course for the fourth time, not helped in any way by a full galeforce wind. It was more a trial of endurance than skill, but eventually Dr. Harris emerged as the winner by two strokes!

Horse riding stables have for many years enjoyed popularity on the Island, and back in the last century Hayling even provided the venue for horse-racing, although it was hardly on a par with Ascot or Epsom. To further the cause of promoting the Island as the Brighton of Hampshire, a grand steeplechase meeting was held in 1834 at Eastoke, but actually it was anything but grand. The weather was so bad that there were hardly any spectators, and even the Grand Ball held in the evening only attracted a total of fifty ladies and gentlemen.

As these races did not set the sporting world alight, another attempt to introduce racing was not made until some thirty years later, July 1867 being the date for Hayling racegoers. Would you believe it, the rains came down once again, so it was just as well that the spectators could shelter in a grandstand that had been erected opposite the Royal Hotel. Seven races took place, and some keen riding took place for trophies that included the Hayling Handicap, the Tournerbury Stakes, and the Hayling Manor Plate. Hayling Races are recorded in the sporting journals as being the racing venue of which Sir Gordon Richards once said "Where?"

Anyone for tennis? When we think of this sport in Hayling we immediately think of the Seacourt Club, and when we think of the Seacourt Club, then we must think of John Marshall. Two of the great passions in John's life were mosquitoes and tennis, and at the former he earnt for himself the reputation of being one of

The Lifeboat Inn in the days when you could drink a pint outside, and feed the chickens at the same time

Regal Cinema and Rose in June, Mengham

The Club, Sunshine Holiday Camp

"Hi-di-hi". Early days at Northney Camp.

Monkey Island and Boating Pool, Beachlands

the foremost authorities in the world, founding the British Mosquito Control Institute at Hayling in 1925. But in addition to swatting mosquitoes he was pretty nifty at swatting tennis balls, and he was responsible for the construction of a real tennis court at Seacourt in 1911, comparable with some of the best courts in the country. John Marshall had organised the construction of his home and tennis court in such a way that he could walk from his house, through the servants quarters, into the music room at Seacourt and reach his indoor real tennis court without having to go outside! He was a pioneer of the game in England, it having originated in France. There were only about ten other such courts in the whole of England at that time in 1911. Marshall had his own professional, Duncan Wilson, who had formerly been at Princes Club in London. Marshall was also a keen entomologist and had built an eleven-roomed laboratory adjacent to Seacourt's real tennis court. He even made his own microscopes.

During the war the entire complex was evacuated and was eventually damaged extensively. The court's glass roof was smashed and laid open to the elements for several years. Charles Silvester later bought the whole estate, converting the enormous house into three separate units and the laboratory into a three-bedroomed house. He repaired the war damage, replacing the glass roof over the court, and progressed to opening the Seacourt Tennis Club with a billiard room, bar and changing rooms. In 1957 it was no longer viable and so he offered the club to members for £4,500 but the sum could not be raised, so it was closed down, staying derelict for seven or eight years. In 1966 Edward "Ned" Danby, who was one of the club's directors, joined forces with Francis Snell (son of Captain Snell) to buy the club. They completely refurbished it, adding several squash courts, badminton courts and a large dining room and bar, making it the successful club it is today. In 1980 Seacourt was listed in the Guinness book of records as being the only place in the world where one could play lawn tennis, rackets, squash, badminton and real tennis all in the one club.

The 1980s heralded the boardsailing invasion of our local waters, and I must confess to being in awe of the dazzling skills displayed by these adventurous folk. But did you know that the sailboard was actually invented in Hayling? If you had thought that America was responsible for introducing this new sport, then you would have been mistaken and just to prove the point Peter Chilvers took the American company Windsurfing International to court over a patents claim, and won the day! It all began on Hayling Island in 1958, when 12-year-old Peter was amusing himself on Mengham Creek. Displaying an inventive mind he constructed a craft from pieces of plywood, a tent fly-sheet, a couple of curtain rings, and a pole. This contraption provided Peter and his pals with plenty of fun in the summer hols, but who would have thought that from such a modest beginning a major new sport would develop to capture the attention of the world? It certainly opened up a new world for Peter Chilvers, for he ventured into the sailboarding business and formed Chilvers Sailboards. And to think it all began at Hayling! Hayling is now the most popular area for sailboarding, especially Northney.

Whilst still on the water, we must not forget that the harbour waters either side of the Island provide excellent conditions for having fun in a small boat. The area has always been able to boast of possessing several fine sailing clubs over the years, catering for this increasingly popular sport.

The oldest club on the Island is the Hayling Island Sailing Club. In the autumn of 1921 seven sailing enthusiasts met to form the H.I.S.C., the rules being based on those of East Cowes club. The first Commodore was Mr. Simkins. The club house was a fisherman's cottage adjacent to Salterns Quay, known as Quay Cottage. Shortly after they moved to premises now occupied by Mengham Rythe Sailing Club. Their first regatta was in 1922 and

The Civil Service Holiday Camp, now Southleigh

the programme included pillow fights on a pole slung between two barges and ended with a mud-pattern race. The original club burgee was designed by R. McKillian, and consisted of an accurate replica of the Hayling coat-of-arms on a red background. Over the years it has been modified. The problem of the extreme tides allowing only three hours sailing each side of a high tide eventually led the club to move house. It was Captain Snell M.C. who realised the potential of the south-eastern tip of Sandy Point. He bought the land and built the foundations of the club on Uffa Fox's wooden canoe shed in 1936. Capt. Ivan Snell's portrait hangs on the dining room wall in the club house today, watching over his creation which has over the years been enlarged and modernised.

Combined Operations Pilotage Parties (COPP) took over the club during the war 1942–5. Landing operations were practised here, the coastline being not unlike the Normandy beaches. Apparently a British landing craft secretly left one night and went over to the French coastline, examined the German landing obstacles erected at sea and pulled aboard about ten of them. They were then taken back to Britain, set up off West Wittering and a group of British soldiers were sent to land there from Hayling to see how they coped.

Today H.I.S.C. enjoys a high reputation for its organisation of World and National Championships, Olympic trials and open events. Other Island sailing clubs today are Northney, Mengham Rythe and nearby Langstone.

One of the first Island pantos took place in the British Legion Hall at Hayling in 1930, this was the spectacular "Robin Hood and the Babes in the Wood", featuring Madame Dorothy's Juveniles. It was much appreciated by an enthusiastic audience and was the start of Hayling's theatrical career.

Entering the realms of straight theatre, I can reveal that the renowned Hayling Players were formed in 1935. Performing at the Victoria Hall their first production was a three-act play called "Baa, Baa, Black Sheep". It was so well received by the audience, that the players were inspired to go on to bigger and better things. That first company included Harry Budd, Vera Carter, Earnest Crawley, Jean Cross, J. Earney, Alan Marshall, Edward Colverson, Herbert Osborn, Elsie Ruffle and Audrey Righton. If there is one lesson that I have learnt as a theatre critic, it is to always mention as many players as you possibly can. It sells papers!

There was a great Scout extravaganza in 1935, "In West Town Tonight", with the Red Triangle Hut ringing to tumultuous applause from proud parents. Scoutmaster Gunnell, take a bow! And we must not forget the Hayling Girl Guides, who were led by their captain, Miss Brabrook. Earlier camp fires were organised during the mid 19th Century, when the Volunteer Camps were held at Hayling with hundreds of residents being attracted to the canteen concerts that were held in the late August evenings, resulting in a jolly good sing-song in which everyone could take part. The camps were pitched in a field close to the Royal Hotel, the last one being held in 1880.

Whilst being entertained in the great outdoors is a wonderful experience on balmy summer evenings, the British climate forces us to retire to the great indoors all too often. So, a meeting hall becomes a necessity. With this in mind, the Victoria Hall in Hayling was opened in July 1898, and of course our old friend Mr. Trigg played his part in the founding of this project. In a speech he stated that the hall would be of benefit to all classes on the Island, and just to prove his point he entertained to dinner at his own expense all the workmen who had been employed in the construction of the hall. The official opening of the Victoria Hall was combined with a benefit for the local life-boat, and attracted a large audience. The proceedings finished with a grand concert that contained a strong nautical flavour, and of the fifteen items presented the most popular was a rousing chorus provided by the entire crew of the Charlie and Adrian lifeboat.

Let us not forget the good folk of Northney; for they had a long battle to get a recreation hall of their own. In fact, villager Mr. Bentley fought for sixty years to get a hall, his pleas falling on deaf ears. The great day eventually dawned in September 1925, however, when the North Hayling Recreation Hall was officially opened, the plans for the building being provided free by Mr. Trigg. Before entering the hall to begin celebrations two trees were planted outside, one of these by Mr. Bentley, who by this time was ninety years old. The villagers of North Hayling did not hesitate in making good use of their new hall, and before long they were dancing all night, sometimes as late as ten o'clock, to the strains of the Hall Orchestra under the direction of Ted Hedger.

There was also plenty of entertainment at the British Legion Hall, opened in Vicarage Lane in 1928 by the Earl of Jellicoe. This was a marvellous achievement, for the Hayling branch had started from modest beginnings in a barn at Mengham House. They also possessed a fine band, and in the 1920's strollers along the seafront were attracted to their open-air concerts in the summer evenings.

The old barn in the grounds of Mengham House was converted into an amateur theatre by Captain Snell after the war. It has been regularly used ever since by amateur dramatic groups and dancing classes. Those were the days when going to the pictures was a regular habit for many. Like the rest of the country, the people of Hayling flocked to the Victoria Hall Cinema for their weekly dose of Charlie Chaplin and Pearl White. This cinema hit trouble in the early 20s for the London Gazette announced that a receiving order for bankruptcy had been made against the proprietor of this cinema, Mr. Francis Marc De La Coze (His real name was probably Fred Hardcastle). But after being closed down all winter, the Hayling Island Cinema re-opened in May, 1922. The building had been re-decorated, new seats installed and lighting improved. Before readers start protesting that there was no electricity on the Island in 1922, I will point out that the management installed their own generators, backed up by accumulators if they should fail. The cinema was described as presenting a handsome appearance, with audiences crammed in for the opening week, the big picture being *One Week* with Buster Keaton supplying the laughs. The proprietor, Mr. P. Brown, was exceedingly pleased with this attendance.

In the 1930s the Savoy Cinema in St. Mary's Road was opened, this was owned by Mr. F. Parmiter. But the cinema that most Hayling folk will remember is the Regal, a modern structure that was opened in December, 1938. This was in the midst of the Golden Years of the cinema, and although crowds flocked into the picture houses in the 40s and 50s in an effort to shake off the wartime blues, another enemy was on the horizon, a little square box that stands in the corner of your living room. The Regal in Hayling closed along with many others of its kind and was demolished in the 1960s. In its place now stands Mengham car park. If one wants to go to the cinema now, the nearest is the Havant Empire, a delightful little picture palace that I hope will remain open despite the present trend. By the way, if cinemas of the past are your pleasure, then I would highly recommend another book in this series *The Cinemas of Portsmouth*.

In those days cinemas were part of the community, and were widely used as meeting halls and venues for special events. Take for anstance the jubilee celebrations of 1935, the Savoy in Hayling was open all day for special children's performances that included a host of marvellously funny cartoon films. All in all, that was quite a day, over 3,000 children from Havant, Emsworth, Waterlooville, Cowplain, and Hayling itself invaded the Island, swarming in by train, charabanc, and bus. Each child

The drapery and outfitting establishment of J.C. Lawrence in Elm Grove. How about a pair of trousers for 2/-?

Turner's Store and Post Office, Elm Grove, Gable Head

was presented with a Jubilee mug, a ticket for tea and six free tickets for the Butlin's Amusement Park. The entertainment also included sports, games, boating and of course the inevitable Punch and Judy.

I have saved the final part of this section of "Leisure and Pleasure" for a popular activity that can be practised by almost anyone over the age of 18, the art of standing at a bar with a glass in your hand. But I prefer to think of public houses from the past not merely as places where one could quench a thirst, but also as meeting places where decisions affecting the community might be made. Halls became available in later years for such purposes, but meetings were not by any means as jolly as the earlier ones held in pubs.

So, let us have a brief look at some of Hayling's palaces of alcoholic delight. The Ferry Boat Inn, formerly the Norfolk Inn" rates as one of the oldest pubs still trading. Since the 18th Century this establishment was the haunt of the watermen who plyed the south-western corner of the Island, and its open doors have been a welcome sight for many thousands of visitors embarking from Southsea in search of sand in the summer months. As I have mentioned in a previous section of the book, the Spraggs family were associated with this inn for many years, in addition to running the ferry service.

In 1933 the Maypole Inn was demolished, and a new building erected further back off the main road, this is the public house we know today. Many local folk were sad to see the old Maypole disappear in 1933, for it had given about 125 years service, being erected in 1808. But even then it was a replacement for a Maypole Inn existed way back into the 17th Century on the same site. It was popular for a gathering called the "May Pole Club", who would assemble once a year dressed in regalia. Led by a band they would march to the parish church for a special service, following which they would return to the pub, generally bringing along with them the Parson, who would preside over a splendid dinner. This was followed by entertainment, providing the local wits and orators a chance to spout at length about stories that had tickled their fancy. Rural life revolved around the old Maypole, so no wonder they were sad to see it's passing in the 30s. But, judging by the number of cars that fill the car park every lunchtime, the Maypole of today also enjoys great popularity.

So also does the Barley Mow, a public house that has been altered extensively over the years, although it began as two cottages. In White's Directory of 1878 it is listed as a beerhouse, with Mrs. Lucy Pannell as the landlady. Lucy was in charge of the Barley Mow when its famous Thrift Club was formed in 1875, the annual share-out being one of the highlights in the Hayling year. The club's golden jubilee was celebrated in 1925 with a special dinner for seventy people, the arrangements being undertaken by the "Mine Host" of that period, Harry Saxby. The original Barley Mow was in Station Road, now Ma Bakers Restaurant, In the 1970s the business was moved to the corner of the same road in what had been a barn in Walters Farm.

Another jubilee event was celebrated on Christmas Day in 1935, this time it was a diamond celebration, for Mr. and Mrs. William Goldring of the Olive Leaf had been married for sixty years. Pride of place on the mantelpiece went to the telegram that had been sent by His Majesty the King, and the regulars drank their health and the King's until the barrels had emptied. The Olive Leaf derived its name from Hayling's first lifeboat, an institution in which the Goldring family played an important part, as mentioned previously. The Lifeboat Inn was built around the same time. The first landlord of the Lifeboat was Richard Smart, who in the 1850s was the proprietor of the Norfolk Lodge Hotel. By the 1870s Mr. Smart had moved on to the West Town Hotel, another hostelry that had been erected in 1867, with a view to enticing travellers disembarking from

Hayling's newly-opened railway system.

I have already mentioned the building of the Royal Hotel, erected in 1826 and included in the aspirations to put the Island on the map. In its shade as it were, the Royal Shades was built at the same time, starting life as the Royal Hotel Tap. Moving eastwards one reaches the Rose and June, another old inn that originally evolved from a cottage. The name of Edward Hunt is associated with this establishment some one hundred years ago, but I expect older readers will be more familiar with the name of William Sharp, who pulled the pints in the early part of this century. Moving to North Hayling, not too far away from the Maypole, we will still find the Yew Tree Inn, another very popular establishment with locals and visitors alike. This pub also dates from the last century, but like so many others of its kind it has been subjected to alterations through the years. More recently the Kittiwake public house was added to the attractions of Eastoke in 1959.

Needless to say, it is not difficult to get a drink in Hayling today, for there is an abundance of hotels and nightspots on hand, and of course holiday centres such as Sinah Warren, Southleigh, Coronation, Northney and Sunshine cater for their visitors' alcoholic needs.

Captain Warner established the first holiday camp at Northney in the mid-twenties. In the early thirties the Civil Service established a holiday camp but it was not a success. Capt. Warner purchased it and re-named it Southleigh. In 1936 a consortium of Portsmouth businessmen built Coronation camp but, like the Civil Service camp, that too was an immediate flop and was sold to Warner. Another Warner's camp was Sinah Warren, originally built as a large residence by Arbuthnot, an outstanding character. It was said he had one of the first battery hen farms. The area which is now Lime Grove and part of Sinah Lane had vast sheds housing poultry in battery cages. The residents around Sinah used to complain of the smell when the wind blew their way over the great manure heaps which built up. He was said to always have plenty of finance to make sure he kept any inspectors quiet. His hen houses always passed the health inspections needless to say. Arbuthnot, who was a millionaire London businessman went to America at the outbreak of the Second World War and never came back. The Royal Navy took it over during the war and afterwards it lay vacant until in 1952 it was sold for £8,000 to a Portsmouth builder who began to turn it into a holiday camp. He sold it to Warners before it was finished however.

The Warner camps came under the capable directorship of the Captain's sons Bill, Alen and John, and remained a family concern until 1982 when they were taken over by Grand Metropolitan Hotels, which I understand is running the camps in much the same way. The Sunshine camp, situated by Pound Corner was started in 1938 but was not finished by the outbreak of World War II. It was offered as a prisoner-of-war camp but was rejected because the accommodation was not considered up to standard! It was eventually used by the Royal Marines. In the late 1970s this camp was used for the filming of one of the saucy "Confessions" series of movies starring Robin Askwith.

"Good Morning, Are You Being Served?"

Unlike many of its surrounding towns and villages Hayling has not really experienced the intrusion of large supermarkets and departmental stores to any great extent and many small shops and businesses thrive.

In the last century there would have been a good chance that the bread the jam was spread upon was supplied by the Barber

Station Road, West Town. Butcher J. Mould next to West Town Post Office

Down at the Ferry Boat Inn

Bakery, for this family business flourished throughout several generations. The bakery was situated in Seafront Road behind Sea View Terrace. Edmund Barber ran the business for many years in the last century, as did Edward during the early part of this one. When Edward Barber died in 1935 at the age of 85, the bakery had been established 122 years. Many of the old food suppliers operated on a dual basis, they were either bakers that sold groceries in addition, or grocers that sold bread as part of their stock. Those who worked in the trade purely as bakers on Hayling, included George Whittington and Hubert Biggs; older readers may recall Hubert's shop in Elm Grove in pre-war days.

Grocers included George Hanson and Flo Watts who kept the villagers of North Hayling well supplied, George Rowe who did the same for Eastoke folk and Harry Woodward who kept shop in West Town. Sam Jones in Ferry Road, Ada Tutchener in Elm Grove and Fred Brown in Mengham Road were other well known names. Ed Wild had formidable competition at Gable Head in the shape of William Pink & Sons, a name most people in the whole of Portsmouth area will recognize. The story of this renowned family grocery empire is very interesting, and is included in another book in this series *Are You Being Served?*

Do you remember when a pound of steak cost 10d? It would almost cost that now for a bag to put it in! If you were to tell the young housewife now that you once paid sevenpence in old money for four lamb chops, she would probably think you were pulling her leg. But that is indeed what you could get for your money in the 20s and 30s. Who provided us with the meat you could eat in the Hayling of old? It could have been Len Twine at his Sea Front shop, or John Mould in Station Road, Jack Hayter or Henry Scarterfield in Elm Grove, Sam Tole at the Sea Front, and not forgetting George Izaacs and his wonderful cooked-meats shop in Selsmore Road. People appeared to eat more fish in those days, this could be bought from the two William's, William Ayling of Elm Grove, and William Seddon in Mengham Road, fishmongers supreme.

Older readers may recall those far off days when there were two milk deliveries a day. All you had to do was put your jug out twice a day and it would be filled as if by magic, or so it seemed. This wonder was really performed by a gentleman who drove a cart through the streets armed with a ladle and churn. The health authorities would not allow this practice now, but I always felt that the milk tasted better then. Hayling milk supplies were provided by Bannister's Dairies of Mengham, Dixon's Dairies in Webb Lane, Fred Dewdney in West Lane, and Ben Turner and Algernon Powell, both in Church Road. The islanders of North Hayling had their daily pinta from either Alf Powell or Ted Twine.

Let us leave these provision merchants and see where the best dressed man or woman would shop in the Hayling of years gone by. If you wanted a pair of trousers for two shillings, then the chap to go and see was James Lawrence in Elm Grove; in fact he sold just about everything, from boots to bath towels. As a young chap James served his apprenticeship at Handley's in Southsea, rising to become departmental manager. He decided to open his own shop in Fawcett Road, Southsea and soon after, added to this a branch at Hayling. After about 20 years he relinquished the Portsmouth shop, and came to reside and work permanently in Hayling, where he also served on the parish council. He had two sons, one being G.C. Lawrence the Hayling auctioneer and estate agent, and the other being J.C. Lawrence of Gosport photographic fame. By the way, most of the postcards of Hayling sold in the Lawrence premises in Elm Grove were taken by J.C. of Gosport, and are now valued collectors' items. When James Lawrence died in 1928 at the age of 80, half of the Island turned out to say farewell. One of the mourners who had particularly fond memories of that old drapers shop was Mr. C. Crassweller, who was one of the oldest employees. His wife, Mrs. Crassweller, was also a staunch member of the Hayling Womens Institute, a worthy organisation that was formed on the Island in 1920.

In those days one went along to drapers such as J.C. Lawrence, or John Andrews of Elm Grove, bought material and took it to be made up by the skilled fingers of dressmakers such as Caroline Samways, Minnie Spencer, Laura Haines or Mrs. King in Station Road. Elm Grove appeared to have been the Mecca for drapers and outfitters, for we can add the name of Charles Herrington, Mary Webb and Elizabeth Instance.

The list of boot and shoe repairers and retailers in Hayling includes Fred Coates of Elm Grove, Emma Hart of the Sea Front, Alf Bruce in Station Road, Alf Kean of Elm Grove, and bootmaker Mark Reeves, a much respected Hayling resident who had the misfortune to meet his end suddenly in 1924 whilst on a shoot in the grounds of Richmond House.

In earlier times, life revolved around tradesmen such as blacksmiths and wheelwrights, men who took a great pride in their work. With so many farms on the Island, these folk made a good living. The list of blacksmiths includes James Hoar, William Kennett, Joe Pannell, and William Rogers. The Hayling wheelwrights included chaps such as George Clinker and Bill Bolton. Some older readers may remember Mr. Bolton, for as well as his old established wheelwright's business, he also served as the caretaker for the Hayling Church of England School for many years. One of the Island smithys used to stand on the corner of Tournerbury Lane in Mengham.

Two of the biggest shops on Hayling today have been in existence for nearly fifty years and deserve a mention here. Pullingers Ltd. started trading in 1935 in Gable Head in premises which are now a stationers shop. In 1937 they moved to their present shop which was built in 1933. During the war they narrowly missed a bomb which dropped in front of the store. On the other side of the road stood a timber framed shop run by G. Hogger. It was erected by a carpenter and was made mainly of wood. The blast of the bomb caused the sides of the shop to collapse leaving the floors intact and the still standing furniture on view to the outside world! After the war, Pullingers re-opened at the same time as Bentley Walker, also of Elm Grove.

So, how about the Hayling Island of today? Hayling has been lucky to escape the ravages of planning that have been inflicted on other towns and villages, helped perhaps by its success in warding off take-over bids from Portsmouth between the 1930s and 50s. Although the "Home Rule for Hayling" banners have been waved regularly through the years while the Island has flourished peacefully enough under the wing of its big brother in Havant, Hayling still remains one of the most pleasant spots on the South Coast where one may live, work, and play. Long Live Hayling!

Acknowledgements

In compiling this book I was fortunate in having the help and encouragement of Nicholas, Roy and Lynda Pine, to whom I give thanks. On the photographic side I would like to thank Mr. J. Smith of Lens of Sutton and David Lawrence, with a very special word of thanks to Alf Harris for letting me dip so freely into his marvellous postcard collection.

Seafront Road, South Hayling. Post Office and Royal Shades, how little it has changed

The Victoria Cinema, Beach Road

The Victoria Café and Hall, Beach Road, formerly the Victoria Cinema. Now the site of Mark Anthony Court